AF243717

LIFE OF EMOTIONS

By: A'NYO JYNNINGS

And

ROBERT LEE YOUNG

younginc24@aol

Life of Emotions

By: A'nyo Jynnings and Robert Lee Young

Cover design by: Anelda L. Ballard

Logo designs by: Andre M. Saunders and Robert Young

Editor: Anelda L. Ballard

Photographs by: Lenny Hamilton and www.istockphoto.com

ISBN 978-0-9768540-4-3

ISBN 0-9768540-4-X

E-mail: younginc24@aol

For Worldwide Distribution. Printed in the United States of America
Published by Jazzy Kitty Greetings Marketing & Publishing, LLC
Using Microsoft Publishing, Adobe and Book Cover Pro Software

ACKNOWLEDGMENTS

Well, the only acknowledgments I have are life, my family, and my friends, because without a bad life there's no greater life to look forward to. Without family, there is no backbone in your life to keep you standing tall as only you can.

Friends are like air, you have good ones and bad ones. The good ones keep you refreshed always and keep you going on to following your dreams. They want you to be the happiest that you can be. The bad ones will see that you are not moving on to a better life. Instead of them thinking, "I will stand by my friend", they will stand by their friend hold back their friend, so they can't achieve what they were destined for.

All I'm saying is, live life everyday as if it was to be your last second. Love everyone and God because with hate in your heart there's no peace. And without peace there's no me. So remember a smile a day will definitely keep stress away.

And thank you for reading my book; I just wanted to acknowledge the fact that I appreciate you. Because without you, this book wouldn't be released, therefore thank you.

I want to thank the staff at Jazzy Kitty Greetings Marketing & Publishing, LLC.

DEDICATIONS

This book is dedicated to my family; my mother Jannette Saylor, my two brothers John Shuntay and Bryan Young, and my sister Monique Young. It's also dedicated to my kids Keyshawn Young, Keith Young and my princess Kaydence Young. Without you nephews and nieces, there is no me. Thank you, Chandra Aikens for encouraging me to write my book.

LIFE OF EMOTIONS

LIFE OF EMOTIONS

INTRODUCTION

This book was written in hopes that my poetry will touch every emotion that runs through the heart. I know that everyone won't, and will never, feel the same; but I guarantee that there's at least one poem that has your name.

MY WORDS, MY THOUGHTS

My words, my thoughts, which you deny

True love that lay at your feet that can disappear,

In less than a blink of an eye

The feelings I share is nothing less than real

If I could, I would mail my heart to you,

In a genuine U.S. Government Seal

And as you open it, a song will play

Saying, "Baby this is my heart and in it you can stay."

Forever or how long you need to,

Because it's here to keep you warm

So that your old love once again become new,

I hereby give you my world My Dear

And everything in it that you can see,

Because I'm deep in space zipping through the stars

Accompanied by nothing, but your love surrounding me

WHEN I THINK OF LOVE

WHEN I THINK OF LOVE
I think of something that's everlasting
If I'm grateful for one thing in this world;
It's your desire for passion

WHEN I THINK OF LOVE
I think of bliss after one taste
I can't stop kissing your warm and loving lips

WHEN I THINK OF LOVE
I can see beauty starring right at me,
Because it takes two hearts for this ship to sail out
Into the open sea

WHEN I SEE LOVE
I see you with me, nothing but unlimited beauty;
And every time we touch, I can feel your heart
And it says…
"YOU'RE IN LOVE WITH ME"

MY ALMOND JOY

It's time for a change, so you should be with me;
To sail under the stars and explore the seas

Together joined to the heart, just you and me
My Chocolate Barbie or should I say MY ALMOND JOY

Kissing your body with nothing but silence, no sound, no noise
I'm addicted to candy and your sweetness is my weakness

I'm hooked, down on one knee with a ring in my hand,
Just ready for your lips so that I can kiss Hershey
And if I should die today, I live with no regrets, no doubts,
Any misgivings or qualms

Whether I'm alive or dead,
Your heart would still rest BETWEEN MY PALMS

YOU CAN BE MY HERBAL TEA

Baby,

All I need is about three kisses from you, okay maybe seven

When you hold me, I just close my eyes;

And picture the stars shinning down on me from Heaven

My Queen,

You're a piece of art like a sculpture but yet you breathe

I hold my chest to feel my heart but it sneaked down to the hand,

That's touching you and relaxed under my

Turtle Neck Right Arm Sleeve

I still appreciate the first day that you came home to me,

That day felt like a breath of fresh air that I needed so much

My knees start to tremble at the first sign of

Your Touch

No it's not a problem; I like it because it's good for me

That just lets me know…

That whenever I get sick,

YOU CAN BE MY HERBAL TEA

FEEL GENUINELY FREE

All I see is beautiful butterflies surrounding me

I'm in a trance called love but still I want to never be free

This feeling is like no other,

It's even taking over the way I breathe

Some say I'm MESMERIZED, just by the way she looks at me;

And I just proudly reply, "Then forever HYPNOTIZED I'll be."

God made people, animals, land,

And even your great grandma's old Orange Tree

In the city we're tied down to the rules of what other men see,

But when I lay in the stillness of your heart's sea

Then and only then,

Do I finally feel GENUINELY FREE

VIOLETS LAST A LIFETIME

On this sunny day I waited for an hour;
To watch the sunset and the birth of a brand-new flower
Your petals pointed up, then they spread out like wings,
And your leaves started turning as mother earth sings

As the day descends, your beauty blossoms;
Like the sun's good-bye rays
I'm watching as your love is planting a seed into my soul,
And forever in my heart you'll stay

I'll repeat my life path again, if you press rewind;
Because if I don't remember anything else,
Its roses may come and go
BUT VIOLETS LAST A LIFETIME

I'LL BLOCK OUT

I'LL BLOCK OUT the noise, cars, then next the crowded bars

Just hanging on the dream of me flying with the stars

I'LL BLOCK OUT lively chats

And kids throwing balls to baseball bats,

And all of the world yelling and arguments

Until I see something that's Heaven-sent

I'll never rush our love because it would last only if it's meant

Meant to be or not to be with someone

That deeply cares for me

I'll give her everything and when there's nothing left

I'll reach down in my soul and give up my last breathe

I'LL BLOCK OUT the world Sweetheart,

Because to me everything is just a great big mess

I will keep on blocking until your heart beat,

IS THE ONLY SOUND LEFT

THREE LETTERS

THREE LETTERS LIKE L.O.V.
Or you can say three words like, "YOU LOVE ME?"

Love can make me but never break me
Sometime it hurts when people say it,
AND THEN FORSAKE ME

Every month, every week, even down to the day;
At night I look upon the stars wishing that love,
WOULD COME BACK MY WAY

My hands they tremble, yearning for your touch;
And my body aches from nights of missing your touch

My heart is like a cell phone, that has unlimited calls
If my money was anything like my love,
YOU COULD HAVE IT ALL

CUPID

CUPID, like a sniper took the shot

From deep within Heavens clouds,

Silence with no sound, but the reaction was pretty loud

As the arrow pierced through my skin,

Something started to merge from within

Within my soul that pumped love to my heart,

Over and over again each time I can see more of the truth,

THAT TORE ME APART

Heaven provided me with a fourth eye to see,

What I've been missing

Your touch, your smell and the taste of you in the kitchen

CUPID was right; your lips are the only lips,

THAT I'M SUPPOSED TO BE KISSING

Yes, the only one for me and if in life I had to lose,

Better yet, if I had to choose between you and the sun,

I guess I would be one DARK SON OF A GUN,

But light would be still shining within the heart,

OF MY CHOSEN ONE

HELLO

Hello there. Hi. How are you?

Oh, Who am I?

I'm the person you call,

When you're feeling down and blue

I'm here to bring exhilaration, delight and cheer;

Every time you smile it brings a piece of my heart near,

Marinating with your soul until it comes to a boil,

Cooking something special as I pull up passionate,

Veggies from with-in your heart's soul

Massaging each one of your touches,

As I caress each kiss

I've been on this earth, 24 years,

AND NEVER FELT MOMENTS LIKE THIS

MY HEART

One o'clock, two o'clock, at three o'clock MY HEART stops

Four o'clock, five o'clock my heart drops

Because the love of my life sees tomorrow, I cannot

She crashed at three and passed at five

She was MY HEART, MY WORLD, MY LIFE

Going through a rough day, she's the reason why I thrive

With my pearl gone, I'm sure to be a clam,

To everyone and everything for my life,

I'm not going to give a Damn

It's over for love and it's over for me,

THE DAY YOU PASSED, SET MY HEART FREE

TO WHOM IT MAY CONCERN

As I sit and write this letter, To Whom It May Concern

I sit back and wonder, what lessons from love I have learned?

I know how to please and keep a smile,

But in return all I get is denial

I can give my all and hand you my heart

But still have this feeling that you're not doing your part

I cook and clean, what more can you ask for?

I see now I'll never be equal to or be enough,

You'll always want for more

So I give to you this beautiful parting gift;

No it's nothing that you can wear and no it doesn't tick

JUST THE THOUGHT OF YOU MAKES ME SICK

CLOUD NINE

Roses are red, violets are blue and sometimes green,

I think of your touch and get lost in your daydream

Your kiss fills me up until I start to feel your caress

I miss the way that you make me feel,

It just makes me want to sing

My heart caters to your soul until loss of breath, death brings,

And I am an Angel of Heaven but I see rapture on earth

So I lay my pride aside and clip my wings

To be with my one true love that gives the meaning to the words,

CLOUD NINE

As we see ecstasy start to come over the horizon,

OUR HEARTS FREEZE IN TIME

I WILL UNDERSTAND

When would you give your heart back to the charity?

When would you finally see the enormous heart,

That's busting out of me?

I can bring you respect and dedication,

Yet you still don't have any trust in me

I could give you the world with all the glitter and gold,

It all means nothing without loyalty

Understand what I say,

Because what I say is from the heart and...Real

How can you say you love someone?

But at the same time my love is just another…Ordeal

Is it such a problem to erase your past and just start over?

For once stop getting drunk on heartless drinks,

And try to stay…Sober

When I lend my hand,

When you're not ready to walk…Heaven's Sand

Just say to me Baby, I'm still on the playground with the boys,

I'm just not ready for a man and I WILL…UNDERSTAND

KING

Close your eyes...Now open them up slowly;

What can you see?

Do you see THE TRUE KING that lies inside Thee?

While we walk hand in hand like birds our hearts fly free

Then disappear unto the sunset like so,

We just let our hearts be

You're a hopeless romantic, well I'm someone deserving

For you, I'll tap-dance on the stage of love,

Until the closing curtain

Through the night I walk with grapes and feel you yearning;

I can please you in many ways but still I keep learning

A KING is someone that shouldn't be afraid of something new

It's a task that I take forward in pleasing,

A QUEEN LIKE YOU

WHY MY HEART WAS BORN

A woman like you that's full of greatness and divine,

I must be out my elegant mind not to ask you to be mine

With juicy lips and curvy hips, with nothing but heart

I'm a Mechanic just in case you start to fall apart

Like crazy glue, I will keep all your pieces together;

And on a rainy day, I'll hover over top of you like an umbrella;

Through the bad weather

I want to be your sunshine through the storm;

I'm your blanket that keeps you comfortable, at ease and warm

I had an intervention when God came to me saying,

Through the breeze I'm the one for you

And you are the one for me

So said the Heavens for you My Love is sworn,

You're the sole reason,

WHY MY HEART WAS BORN

MAGIC

Our hearts are like Tinker Bell and Peter Pan
Flying around with nothing but love and Magic Sand,
Promise each other to never, ever, ever let our love…
GROW OLD AGAIN

I'm a man that needs more but never scared to settle for less
If your lungs My Queen would ever start to suffocate,
I WOULD LEND YOU MY BREATH

Think of life as this, a staircase going up,
And love as a mystic magic power
THAT WIZARDS KEEP ON TUCK

Your loyalty and personality is something that,
MONEY AND DIAMONDS CAN'T BUY

Did I mention that you adore all of my attention?
When I kiss down your back until I reach your thighs,
Then I pull out my tongue,
AND SAY SURPRISE!

WE DON'T TALK

WE DON'T TALK anymore,
All we do is argue, bicker and fight;
You don't even touch me anymore

As we lie together on the same bed,
Such an uncomfortable feeling
Lying with a woman full of spite,
So I get up and sleep on the couch for the night

I work over thirteen hours a day,
And then I have to come home to cook and clean
Every day at quitting time,
I get this feeling of such disappointment
And I have to concentrate to breathe

Just knowing that I'm coming home to someone,
That focuses on nothing but just being mean

(Continued)

WE DON'T TALK

Anger builds up from your heart;
That stretches down to your sleeve

You know what?
Before this situation gets worse,
I THINK THAT I SHOULD LEAVE

And since you're so materialistic,
You can keep everything that was given from me

You can keep the house, the furniture and the car
As a matter of fact,
HERE ARE THE KEYS!

I refuse to love someone,
THAT MAKES ME LIVE ON MY KNEES

TRUE LOVE I WOULDN'T KNOW

When I'm hurt I cry, when I'm cut I bleed,
WHEN I'M IN PAIN, THAT'S ALL I FEEL

As I dwell in the belly of my unforgiving sorrow,
MY HEART BEGINS TO TURN INTO STEEL,

To endure such pain, I have to be much more than strong;
The only thing that keeps me going is hearing your voice,
THROUGH LOVE DEVOTED SONG

I dreamed of this day to come far before my life has begun,
On the day that you were born our hearts formed an eclipse
AND MERGED WITH THE SUN

I start to caress your hands as my lips continued to kissing,
YOUR AFFECTIONATE SOUL

For 24 years, my heart was never complete
Until the day you came into my life and converted my
HEART-WHOLE

And it was your essence that my body consoled
Without your guidance,
TRUE LOVE I WOULDN'T KNOW

MY SCULPTURE

I am forming this sculpture, chiseled to the tee;

Incising every flaw that my eyes can see

After I carve out your lips,

Then a notch for a nose to breathe

Then here comes two beautiful eyes,

So that you can gaze across the seas

I'm sculpturing no ordinary or average woman

This lady don't have to be astonishing,

But at least be extraordinary

You don't have to be Cinderella to be mine, I indeed take fairies

Just have faith in me and my passion, Dearest

And don't be afraid to take risks

Jump into my heart's soul and give it a passionate kiss

MY SCULPTURE is almost complete,

I polished the top and now I'm refining the feet

One kiss from my lips would turn my sovereign real,

And bring her alive on this day, I give up the games,

AND TURN YOU MY SCULPTURE INTO MY WIFE

FOR ETERNITY

I'm not loving you like I need to

I choose the wrong path each day,

And now I'm looking pitiful

Sadness rains inside me as sorrow,

Takes its place in my heart

Is this really love or is it lust?

Running through me like the spear of a dart

These memories was made in the coldest winter

My trust is all used up, this relationship is equal to,

Fried B.S. with a side of waste of time for dinner to simmer;

In the pot of ungratefulness heading in the opposite

Direction of bliss

What can I do to make up for the lack of a man?

Should I pull myself up by my colorful threads…?

To prove that I still care?

I race the falling star through Heaven's night,

UNTIL I REACH THE CRASH SITE

(Continued)

FOR ETERNITY

To see that your extremely rare heart is still waiting there;
So I bend down on one knee,
Then notice your hand reaching for me

So I take it and place it upon my heart,
And say this is our bond and this is our trust,
Will you forgive me?

Don't say YES or NO right now, just say MAYBE;
But I want to share this night with you My Love...
FOR ETERNITY

SLIP INTO PARADISE

As our minds SLIP INTO PARADISE,

And our hearts beat together in harmony

My body moves in closer as your faith starts to believe in me

With tears in your eyes and desperation in my heart,

Pleading with you to stay and do your part

And in my heart you'll settle

I love the way you trust me to,

Touch on your roses as I'm kissing on your petals

The feeling gets so good that I stick my tongue out,

And start licking on your meadow's way

Licking on your temple, pleasing your body

From January to December

Proving to you My Lady each day,

Why your love that exists in my heart should stay

(Continued)

SLIP INTO PARADISE

Sex and Making Love is far from the same

Making Love is superb, delicate as I kiss your lips,

And say your body is very tasteful

But sex is very intense

Flipping your body up and down,

As your nails pierced my skin, as I screamed your name

Our love is not confidential, nor excruciating

Because as you sail...
OUR SOUL'S SEAS

As I make sure both hearts concentrate,

On elevating away from...
THE WORLD'S STRAIN

ETERNITY SEND

All these males are like juice over the tip of the cup!

Just remember I'm your last sip,

They can kiss on your softest spot but only I focus on the tip

I'm so good that you'll have to check into rehab

Because Baby I'm your ecstasy

I can write a million words about you,

But they will all mean the same thing to me

A passionate kiss leads to passionate crimes;

As we toast hearts and our souls sit,

And admiring affectionate times

Tender gentle violets float through love's cloudy valley;

I'm embracing all the compassion that's beneath your arms

Searching for love, My Lady you don't have to be alone;

I'll be your light in your heart's dark alley

Over friendship mountaintop through your waterfalls peak,

I can be your Super Mario, just let me fix your leak

Or we might just need to escape deep into space just for the weekend

It's good to finally experience True Love,

THAT COULD ROLL OVER INTO ETERNAL SEND

YOU IGNITE MY FIRE

YOU IGNITE MY FIRE within my insight,

To taste your love Baby, I just might

I see you smile as we walk through the park

I'm racing time for love,

So that I can see the finish before the start

I can be the light that shelters the dark

I take the pieces that are broken apart,

And place them back together to form your heart

Your soul is another story that needs to be told,

Because everything that glitters, sure isn't gold

But I am unique,

So I say that I'm a diamond just waiting to be unfold

I am like the calm that embraces you after the storm,

Where I am from showing exceptional love is the norm

Just give me a chance to let my heart be the vaccine

FOR YOUR SORROW'S SCORN

PERPETUAL BLISS

My days are lost with no tomorrow,

And my nights are filled with all the Angels' sorrow

A smile of cheer might let me just crack a smirk,

Because no matter what I do, my insides still hurt

In the meantime, in between time, you use to say to me;

"Don't let negative vibes cloud your judgment;

For you are my Man and I'll forever be your Lady."

Then I'll reply, "You're not just my Guardian Angel

You're more than Heaven-sent."

This relationship is not just our destiny,

It was packaged that God Himself assist

As the scenic clouds shelter our hearts,

We rely on the stillness of time to remain in

PERPETUAL BLISS

SING A LOVE SONG

The night is gone; as the morning is young

I bend over between your legs,

And play alarm clock with my tongue

Your mouth moans as your hands roam and your carcass (body) squirm,

I suck on your lips as your body I start to learn

As you reach your max, I begin to climb your temple

Proving to you that Making Love can be this simple

Front, back, even side to side as you ride

You sit on top of my lap as we release together,

As I stay attached inside

Then I lay you back slowly and massage your feet,

And thank you for your love and being so sweet

You taste like honey but now it's time to eat

I made you breakfast in bed, as you thank me for head,

Today will be continue incessant even after we are wed

So take my hand My Queen,

And let's dance with the stars really soon

Other men can take you to the clouds but my heart can lift you up

TO SING A LOVE SONG WITH THE MOON

IF I WERE TO EVER FALL IN LOVE

IF I WERE TO EVER FALL IN LOVE,
Hearts will rain down from the Heaven's cradle
AND OUR SOUL RACES TO BECOME STABLE

My Significant Other, yes that's what you are
Me without you is like envisioning the night,
WITHOUT EVEN ONE STAR

On lonely nights my imagination gets the best of me;
But it's the only time that my heart and brain,
TRULY JUST LET EVERYTHING RUN FREE

As pleasant thoughts clutter my mind but not my judgments
I'm visualize juicy passionate kisses,
THAT FELT HEAVEN-SENT

Love is a cosmos that very few journey the tour
People are so in a rush to feel loved,
And end up with lust knocking at their door
Some only come for one thing,
YOUR BODY TO EXPLORE

But not My Sweetheart, she does more then make me grin
Because she's smart and knows the rules that protect us from sins
Before we share virtue,
WE MUST FIRST CONTRIBUTE TO BEING FRIENDS

WHAT IS PERFECTION?

WHAT IS PERFECTION?
Perfection is a kiss without any words,
Realization of hearts fluttering like birds

Perfection is reaching your climax without one touch,
Perfection is coming home to someone that loves you so much

What can perfection truly do for me?
Perfection let me focus offshore to see true beauty;
Perfection has no worry or fear,
It just let great things be

Perfection is not only encouragement...
IT'S REASSURANCE OF LOYALTY

MEAN THE WORLD TO ME

We been through it all from heart evictions,
Down to our mental sorrows turning our facts to fiction

No more arguments and no more shame,
No more frustrated nights and no more strain

Let's empty out our past until nothing remain
I know the feeling first hand, from heartache and pain
But those women in my past,
You and them is far from being the same

Why be his option,
When you can be my heart's priority?
You see, please stop letting him treat you like an individual,
When you can walk into my heart,
AND MEAN THE WORLD TO ME

WHERE YOU STAND

Before commute can set in,

I have to know WHERE YOU STAND

If you're ready for something eternal,

Then give me your hand

I take this ring of trust and emit it to you,

Because I believe whatever problems that await us

We are strong enough to work through

What is caring without love and love without a friend?

Marriage isn't a phase that you go through,

It's where you and your spouse make a stand

It's a tough road to the finish line,

But we can help each other through any situation,

With a smile that started by grinning;

All we have to do is take it one day at a time,

My soon to be wife

AS WE START STEP-BY-STEP FROM THE BEGINNING

SAYING GRACE

Here I stand on top of Holy Land,
Dear God, Please forgive me for as though I had sin
I take full responsibility of my actions,
I JUST HOPE THAT YOU UNDERSTAND

As rain falls outside and hit the tip of my Window Sill
I think of you and how you taught people how to appreciate,
The Little Things

Even the ones that you knew were going to betray you
AFTER THE LAST MEAL

So I forgive all the people that treated me wrong,
And threw my name in the dirt
But if you sit back and think about it,
I'M NOT THE ONE THAT YOU REALLY HURT

Optimistic as I must be to live in this life
I still thrive for greatness,
BEFORE MY SPIRIT FROM MY BODY DESERTS

I don't look for material things or even try to play it safe;
You only get one chance at life, so enjoy your space
Life can be magnificent if before every deed
YOU SAY 'THANK YOU' BY SAYING GRACE

I GUESS THAT'S ME

I'm pompous, selfish and inpatient…Yeah, I guess that's me?

My arrogance is a disease that spreads, bringing conceitedness;

Every time you inhale, you breathe in Thee

If you don't like my attitude,

And think that I'm not kosher and my behavior is rude

Awe shows in your face because now you have nowhere to go

You cheated on me and left me for him,

And he just left you feeling like a 'Ho'

I see confusion in your eyes, as you shed each tear

But I don't understand why you left me alone

That means Sweetheart that you don't really want to be here

So pick up your bags and the rest of your stuff

I have some more of your things,

I hope that it all can fit in your truck

But personally the more I think about it, life with you really sucks

It's because of your dishonesty that my heart feels bankrupt

But you will only be my past and that's where your pain will stay,

Because I know better than to you corrupt, my new Lady

KISSING YOU SOFTLY

Kissing you softly as the sunrise upon the sea
Our eyes lock as we both breathe the coolness of the fan's breeze,
As your gentle touch starts to take over me

As your tender soothing hands caresses down my temple,
I began to think maybe MAKING LOVE can be this simple

Passion marks leave a trail down your body,
Until I reach your G SPOT
As my tongue rushes around in a circle firmly,
You silently whisper, 'DON'T STOP!'
Then I kick it into high gear until your climax drops

Your hands massage the top of my head, as if you was saying thank you
I come from the South up to your New York Twin Towers
My mouth makes a crash landing,
AS YOUR FIRM NIPPLES GET DEVOURED

Inhaling your smell and consuming the immensity of your taste,
As we try not to rush and make haste

We rapidly slow down the moment,
Because we know that time can wait
As I'm MAKING LOVE to my special someone,
We turn off the world as we mate

LOVE'S NAME

I used to care, now I could care less;

Because dealing with someone like you

Brings no happiness, JUST STRESS

What's the point of this relationship, if there's no gain?

Just the feeling of a migraine that's imprinted in my brain,

And I lost the feeling of love and now it beats with a strain

No matter how hard I try,

Our relations will never again be the same

I must admit I have real love for you and that will not change

But we can't keep pretending,

That we still live together in LOVE'S NAME

We know that not even a drop of feelings for the other remains

Let epoch (age) go on and let change bring

Or we both going to be going through,

THE SAME DAMN THING!

WE WOULD ALWAYS BE A PAIR

One year has passed but yet I still have not cried,

Two years has passed for me to start to feel sorrow inside

Three years has passed and I knew that I could no longer deny;

The feeling that I wish that it was me,

That jumped in front of you and died

I have the same dream each night,

Oh no, they're nightmares

My mind keeps going back to that dreadful day,

When the killer took your life

And I was so scared my body was frozen;

But that didn't stop my stare

As your body rushed to save me,

As the sound of the burrow popped

At that same moment my heart slowed down,

Right before it dropped

I didn't know whether to chase the man or give you my air

When your breathing stopped

(Continued)

WE WOULD ALWAYS BE A PAIR

This situation was my entire fault,
I played the best friend role too long
When all this time you could of had my heart

And now you're gone in what we hope is a better place
On the fourth year, I understood each and every nightmare
My pride was so overwhelming, as if I didn't care

But now I finally understand what you were telling me
Whether you're here in flesh or not,
WE WOULD ALWAYS BE A PAIR

A NIGHT LIKE NO OTHER

On a night like no other
Where you see nothing more than closed doors,
And broken shutters

Drastic times when people from different backgrounds meet
A teenager comes in to rob the store clerk to take a few dollars,
For something to eat

Forty-four in hand, hoping if something jumps off;
The gun don't jam

Then a distraction took the youngster's eyes off the stand,
And the next thing he knew the gun was pointed
At the wrong man

Two shots accidentally went off into the grown man's skull
Paranoid to reality and what he just saw;
He turned around and decided to kill them all

This Foster Child, to think with logic did not even bother;
He felt like committing suicide after finding out that…
ONE OF HIS VICTIMS WAS HIS BIOLOGICAL FATHER

SAY THAT YOU LOVE ME

When I start to think that I'm down and out,

And began to give into sorrow's power

I then close my eye lids shut and count down the universal hours

Until the time I feel the embraces of your arms.

Feeling me with April Showers

A good day can go bad,

As well as happiness can very quickly turn sad

But if you just have one person,

That can lend you just a piece of their time

Can change the unpleasant parts of your past,

With one kiss that can rewind and make sure that this love lasts

This relationship may be new,

But remember nothing in this life is a guarantee

To keep me going all you have to do each day is,

SAY THAT YOU LOVE ME

MY MIND BECOMES STILL

When my mind becomes still
And my vision seems to fade
Instead of the bad,
I focus on the positive choices that I have made

Unpleasant days I know no more
Only blissful late night conversations as we talk upon the phone,
And finish in nothing but I love You's and I love you Too's
Keeping each other away from feeling hatred
And the rain of mourning blues

Present some of the greater things in life are unseen
That's why you close your eyes when you kiss, cry,
Or dream of Thee

It's 4 am and I can't sleep until I feel your tender caress,
Consuming me

Taking away all of my tears, fears and pain;
I need you like fresh air down to the blood in my arm vein
As your heart insists on compelling,
MY LOVE THE SAME

IMAGINE

IMAGINE...If words were making love on my planet,

But words I never saw

Only kissing and affection then passion conquered all

IMAGINE…If there were no worries,

Yet blissful morning dreams

But sometimes making love isn't always what it seems,

We can make love at your office while you type today,

Just say Baby I love you over the phone,

I took your breath away

As you sat in your chair wanting to drift to me,

Because my heart is always on your mind

Instead of hate it's my love you see

SO IMAGINE…This then come and visualize that

IMAGINE…That you became my better half,

And now believe in no turning back

CLOSE YOUR EYES

Just close your eyes and think of me,

Just imagine all the ways that I can set you free

Your heart don't have to wonder no more,

Just set its temperature on me

Love can learn you, and just the way you are,

Love can keep you or lift you with the stars

Seven worlds cannot be enough for the love that I have for you,

I breathe in the clouds in the skies until my soul turns blue

Violets falling from the Heavens,

Just because of the look in your eyes

You're more than just my life

YOU'RE THE REASON WHY I THRIVE

I STAY AWAKE

In my mind I stay awake with dreams stuck inside

Holding hands while walking,

And kissing as we board Heaven's ride

I wish upon a star to find my heart's peace,

Pretending all the sound that was around me had ceased

Everything disappear until the only thing left is,

You standing in front of me

In my mind the world has no negative parts

Violets are my guns and roses are my sharks,

And you don't need to be scared

When you're walking in the city after dark

Because in my mind the heart didn't form inside the body,

THE BODY FORMED AROUND THE HEART

CARAMEL BROTHER

I'm a cool Chocolate Caramel brother,
I can be your best friend, confidante and your love's sky blue
See this is my vision that I can see it so clear

Your eyes connect with mine,
And at that moment find something true
As I move, you move in the way that I want you to

Dancing with Heaven until we turn the past,
Back to something new for you to see
What we have is real enough for my heart to contribute to you,
You stay FAITHFUL to me

Our souls sail into the Eternal Heaven's significant seas,
And our hearts will flow with
PROMINENT STAR'S BREEZE

IF I HAD ONE WISH

If I had one wish, what could it be?
If I had one wish the first thought would be,
YOU AT HOME ALONE WITH ME

If I had a second wish now,
That one would be the best of all
My second would be to get intent in your heart's world,
AND FOREVER FREE FALL

If I had a third wish now that's tricky let me see,
Oh never mind because my wish has already came true

In the future you'll be married to a King,
And entrapping his heart
AND YOU WILL SET HIS SOUL FREE

YOU'LL BE MY WIFE

This is no poem or any kind of poetry;
This is just to let you know how much you mean to me

My mouth has no words that can be spoken,
But my heart fixed itself because with you,
It can never be broken

The way we touch even down to our intimate kiss,
I would pay the world to keep Experiencing   (blissful) Moments
like this

You're my best friend, down to my lover you see
I don't ask for much,
I just ask for me to love you and you to love me

I know that we have much to learn about one another's lives;
But all I ask is to promise to never treat me like your enemy,
AND VOW THAT ONE DAY YOU'LL BE MY WIFE

HEAVEN'S ANGEL OF LOVE

Heaven's Angel of love is now on earth

I'm tired of these so-called men giving you less than your worth

See my life is very simple;

The goal is to take one heart and push it to delineate

The look into her beautiful round eyes with no organ,

Her mind you penetrate

My heart is an entire ocean of emotion that's

Enlightened to swim in

Never bragging just letting you know my passion for you is,

So Strong that my words should go down in history

As the eleventh sin

I can stand in the middle of the ocean,

And still have a forest full of feelings and thoughts

Both trapped inside my silhouette

See if you contemplate on it long enough,

You can see yourself surfing on my love's life line on the daily,

As if it was the Worldwide net

You see my lady no material things to offer at all,

But I can submit to you friendship, passion, true love and respect

ONE KISS, ONE HEART, ONE STAR

ONE KISS can bring a smile to your wife,

ONE HEART can change her life

ONE STAR can brighten the night,

As the moon's horizon brings to our eyes beauty's sight

You can propose to her a hundred times over, in many ways;

But there's only one proposal that can make her stay

To some, the words "I LOVE YOU"…is just a thought or game,

But to me, love is like going across country on a train

If I had a choice between living forever,

Or just one night with you know who…

I would have the best night ever,

IN HEAVEN WITH YOU

IF I WERE TO LOSE EVERYTHING

If I were to lose everything in one week

I would move away from drama,

Until I reach the paradise and peace I seek

If I were to lose my house, my car, even my entire bank roll

I will pick up the rest of my stuff,

And finish out my harmony's stroll

Within the next two days,

I'll lose the beautiful fantasies of you in my mind;

And as the last thought runs dry,

My heart will stop itself to cherish the exquisite times

My life is going fast and I have not much longer to last

So I get down upon my knees in a magnificent groove,

And pray to God that your love would be the last thing

THAT I LOSE

GOOD-BYE MY LOVE

Good-bye My Love, I'm saying farewell to this world;

Hello My Love, can you take care of this gift, My Girl

The gift of love, pleasure and passion

The gift of your touch feeling like it's Heaven sent,

So show me love, if you'll be more than just My Girl

I'm looking for realities Queen not the one you see in…
Your Dreams

The one that I'll love to see smile as we sail down…
Paradise Streams

Well, let me break it down so that you can see what it is…
That I Mean

What we have is more than just being friends

Were at the fork in the road,

One way is love and the other is toward…
A Best Friend

I say just walk in the middle so that our heart's eternal purity…
Can Begin

IS REAL LOVE FICTION?

Roses are red; violets are purple and blue

IS REAL LOVE FICTION?

Or can it really become true?

Can fireworks fly, as we lay down one kiss?

If we don't touch for the day, can your feelings be missed?

If the moon blows out, can I still see my star shine?

I wonder is it wrong to fantasize about your heart being mine

We are from two very different worlds,

But at the same time merge into one

I am your night and you are my life, my world and my sun

Our love is more then the birds and the bees

You are my rose and I'm your violet,

Together were entwine as one blowing through the breeze

MY REASON FOR LIFE

With you, my tears have no beginning

Without you, my tears have no end

Each time a thought comes about you, I arise

I dream of kissing your soft lips,

As I gaze into your eyes

Look a here My Dear, I can't last on this world forever

But what I can do is take my heart,

And plant it beneath the ground

And up will grow a tree full of love,

To protect you from the rainy weather

You are more then what meets the eye,

Because you are My Love, My World

AND MY REASON FOR LIFE

AS YOUR ROSE BLOSSOMS

A black rose is a symbol of being hurt,

So for your black rose, I'll plant it in Heaven's soil;

With my heart to replenish the dirt

Developing trust minerals and passion leaves

And as your rose blossoms you can share,

Your love's pollen with all the birds and bees

So that your stem can dance with the delightful breeze,

And as ecstasy arises, joyful bliss will plant true love trees

The world is guaranteed to hurt you,

BUT YOU WOULD NEVER GET THAT FROM ME

FELL IN LOVE

I looked into your eyes,
And found your beautiful smile

I looked into your heart,
And found your magnificent love

I looked into your soul,
And found Heaven's light

I looked at all of the things that I adore,
And tripped and fell in love with you once more

If the Heavens had eyes, it would be you they see;
Slipping and sliding until you lose your balance,
AND FELL IN LOVE WITH ME

TRUE LOVE

True love only comes in one lifetime;

Some people take advantage of it

And destroy their own love line

True love is confidential in all of its sense,

I found my emotion starting five and lust is on the bench

Life seems as if it's fleeting, so fragile is love once is found,

But love is like the TV remote it's not easy to find

It's as if you're searching for a single red rose,

In a field of roses on the ground

To leave it unattended,

It wilts and dies, never to be revived

Until you lay upon one petal,

A SINGLE KISS TO BRING LIFE

I AM FREE

Look in the mirror and repeat after me,

I love you, I need you and you're beautiful to the eyes

When negative things arise I would keep pushing,

On toward positive vibes without asking why

I love myself, so to be in love

I need not thrive to be in just for other eyes to see

It's okay to be alone at times,

And wait for that person that loves me for me

I look here at my reflection and smile,

Because from all negativity…I AM FREE

LISTEN TO MY WORDS

Listen to my words and believe they are true

I'm the winner of many and who will lose?

I guess you

Tomorrow will be the day

When your heart gets taken away,

By someone that's just waiting to make your day

A Yo A'nyo in winning, he'll lead and you will follow

He might be a model but you're the genie in his heart's bottle

Fight for My Queen, I should as pride I swallow

My dream home is your heart

Look at this; I can build you a model see…

The goal is to be your dream man,

And I can't, if when times get hard I just pick up and leave

Because a King is known for being,

THE BEST THAT HE COULD BE

WASHING AWAY PAIN

I need to wash away all of this pain,

That's implanted beneath my brain

Looking for more in life than the tears that I cry,

I'm looking to be in a world full of nothing

But roses and butterflies

And in Heaven's Valley where violets lie,

Just a peek of your smile can brighten the darken nights sky,

Drenching me full of love which in my heart is the same,

THESE ARE THE BLESSINGS OF WASHING AWAY PAIN

THE GOOD LIFE

The Good Life is inspired by love and guided by knowledge
Life is like an onion:
You peel it off one layer at a time and sometimes you weep
With tear drops of negativity dropping to your clothes and seep

Until a blemish arises and for the rest of your nights will stay
You don't get to choose how or when you're going to die,
You can only decide how you're going to live today

They say when life gives you limes, you should make limeade
But all my limes are rotten,
I guess I'm cursed by the past decisions I made

When I look in the mirror, all I see is failure
As a son, brother, man and father,
I look at achievement and say why even bother

All my life all I wanted to do was please others and see them smile
And appreciate the things I do
But the same people that I tried to please turned their back on me
Who knew?

I give my all into going out my way to be a good person,
But in return all I can get is stress and conflict
I guess this is my sad life no matter how hard I try,
I JUST CAN'T FIX IT

SEDUCE LOVE

Seduce Love in all the ways that you see fit,

Take advantage of my tongue as it vibrates your Clit

Seduce me in ways that people only dream of,

In the darkest places beneath their brain

Seduce me My Lady during Christmas winter,

Or between the drops of the summer rain

It's starting to be clear to me,

Baby that you love what I can do

Seducing your mind as we talk on the phone

And seducing your body as my fervent parts,

Connect inside of you

In my mind pleasing you, just sets my soul completely free;

Because it is you that seduced the loving heart,

THAT SITS INSIDE OF ME

HERE I STAND

Here I stand, in front of me
As my eyes wander, I am the only thing that I see

When I move, you move in just the same way
I hold out my hand but notice in yours it's my heart at bay

So I turn around in place and clap my heels,
And I look up to see your lips start to become unsealed

And a smile is born for my heart to see
As your touch starts to make me feel more sacred
As I'm dancing with your soul under the star's seas

Love tension begin to build from inside of me,
Like a finished recipe

Because I know that my feelings are not alone anymore,
As I am free

For sure as in this life and the next, I'm a reflection of you;
AND YOUR LOVE IS A REFLECTION OF ME

YOUR EYES

There was something in your eyes I noticed as I passed bye
So I slightly turned around and become aware of more,
Then what lie beneath your thighs

I run up to you and grab your hand,
As if it was my way of saying 'Hi'
I brought you closer to me and said,
"My heart knows you from its past life."

I can tell by the glow that sparkles in your eyes;
This feeling that I feel right now,
You couldn't get it even if you were the only one in the world
That could fly

Look, let's try to take our past love,
And in it bring out refine
I don't want your body,
JUST YOUR MIND FROM TIME TO TIME

AMOUR

AMOUR is as easy as 1, 2, 3
If you don't remember the directions,
Then just come and follow me

LOVE is spoken in many languages,
And has many lessons for your mind to see

No matter if it's mentioned in the winter, spring or fall,
Through life blizzards, LOVE will answer your heart's call

When our pockets are going through rough times,
LOVE will help our hearts feel wealthy to the tee

Three centuries may pass as our hairs twirl to gray seas
But MY LOVE will still remain the same,
JUST LIKE THE LOVE YOU HAVE FOR ME

WE BOTH FEEL THE SAME

How I feel you feel, we both feel the same
Together forming true love, as seen in Jesus' name

We push away from the world,
And in space we build a planet full of love
And in it, we will remain

A world without lust, strain or pain,
Sadly to say, this world only exists in my heart;
As it sends pictures of your beauty to my brain

EMOTIONAL HEARTS

From the moon to the stars,
What a sight of you swinging from the Heaven's bars
EMOTIONAL HEARTS forming a line like funeral cars

To measure the love that we have,
You will have to be on Mars to see

I place your heart in my hands and crush it,
Then breathe in your debris
Have your love run through my veins as a part of me
Having our heart become separated from one to form three

Three hearts, two minds stuck in the center of time,
To remain until 200 heart beats plus nine

When I am alone, she tells me that she loves me;
By giving me that special tingle
BENEATH MY SPINE

MY HEART'S DESIRE

When the earth rains fire,
As your love be MY HEART'S DESIRE

And the oceans waves wash up just along the bay,
You step into my heart and in there your trust stays

Each step that I take in this life form
I will realize no matter how hard it rains,
The sun will always shine after the storm

So I vow to My Love never again will she feel harm,
Because now she's protected,
BY MY HEART'S HOME SAFETY ALARM

LIPS OF ROYALTY

I think you're lying when you say that you need me
In the back of my mind your words are too good to be true

But in my heart it's like all that you're saying is,
"New for my eyes to see."
I mean finally, love knocks at my door,
Can this really be?

A Queen blessing me with her presence,
As she stands in front of me
KISSING ME WITH LIPS OF ROYALTY

I JUST CAN'T LET IT GO

Another life lost to the misery of the streets,
Cowards thinking of their short term life, all over some beef
He's over there making money,
So I need to catch him with this Heat

The Snake snuck up behind him,
And shoots him in the back of his head
As the bullet escapes through his teeth
Oh he screwed My Girl, all boy we got beef

Another Young Nigga dead from the dumb crap in the streets
He was seventeen years old with no diploma selling gold
But they're Haters everywhere walking with no soul

The block is not for you young boy, this is a grown man's game,
We hurt our families with no shame

I love my life even if the money starts to come in slow,
All my friends are dying around me
But I'm too attached to the street life
And as dumb as it sounds, I JUST CAN'T LET IT GO

THE DEFINITION OF HAPPINESS

I had a dream last night;
It was such a thing for the eyes to see
Honestly, I can actually feel your kisses touching me

Feeling like massaging strokes from the warm sea currents
As I hear "I LOVE YOU" from the whispering wind breeze

I really don't know what has came over Thee
My heart was in the right place and my soul was set free

I guess for that brief moment I dreamed,
That you were in love with me
And for once the definition of happiness,
I KNEW TO BE

YOU CAN LEAVE JUST AS QUICK

I was excited because I was falling in love with you
Now that I have fallen,
I can't believe the B.S. that you put me through

I cook and I clean but yet you do nothing but sit on your Ass
Even when I'm tired and get off from work,
I have to come home to over filled trash

I guess just because I say that you're My Queen
I'm just supposed to kiss your Butt,
You got me messed up

Where I am from, showing love isn't a crime
I thought you would have been the one to appreciate,
The wine and dine

But my love for you is starting to feel like an hour glass;
You know sooner or later it's going to run out of time

So go ahead to your girlfriend's and talk your Bull,
You and this relationship makes me sick
Just know as easy as you came into my life,
YOU CAN LEAVE IT JUST AS QUICK

SOUL MEETS SOUL

Soul meets Soul on top of lovers' lips,
As my hands become joined at your hips

Holding your body close to me,
So that I can feel your heart squirm
And new love in all of its being, I can fully learn;
One kiss to open your heart and the third for me to earn

As I patiently wait to hear your loving words of grace
I take a moment to gaze at our future in its presence,
At this moment taking place

So I ask one question that will change our lives for here and now,
As each life curve
As your heart plants itself inside of me,
And becomes my body's main nerve

Will you cherish me?
Come on, let's be more than any eyes can see?
So on this beautiful day,
Will you marry me, on top of love's open seas?

WHEN YOU LOVE SOMEONE

When you love someone,
All your saved-up wishes start coming out

So more of your love I can earn
The greatest thing you'll ever learn,
Is to love and be loved in return

You will never know true happiness,
Until you have truly loved

And unfortunately you will never understand,
What pain really is until you have lost love

And without it, from there on you have to continue to live,
Without a heart, just a lonely empty soul

WHEN THE SUN GROWS COLD

When the sun grows cold,

And the stars grow old

I can be the last man on earth,

But still treat your heart like it's pure gold

Love is like war,

Easy to begin but hard to end

A day without it, feels like Eternity in sin

God wakes you up every morning of each day,

To gamble your emotions for a free chance to

DOUSE IN LOVE'S BAY

WHAT IF?

WHAT IF…

Love was as simple as just saying the words?

WHAT IF…

People would cherish what they have?

Instead of during hard times fly south like hollow birds

WHAT IF…

The sky was all blue with no signs of cloud nine?

Would you still appreciate this pure passion of mine?

WHAT IF…

Roses were a symbol of love's cry?

Would that be the reason why after a few days they die?

WHAT IF…

Love was perfect with no assist?

WHAT IF…

Life felt perfect, like the precise moment that we kissed?

Would you want to change anything?

As my heart makes your mind a Romanticist

I FLOAT ON THE CLOUDS

I float on the clouds, when your name comes to mind,
Smelling your sweet scent through the breeze of time

My cologne lingers in the air as I open up your thighs,
And you, I pardon

All I hear is oh; we can't, what if…
Oh Baby as my mouth open just as my
Private hardens

And the words of my tongue start traveling the roads to your
Secret Garden

Your words then become just a complete blur,
As I enjoy massaging my lips against your soft mink fur

To not please My Queen, is like not knowing how to smile;
My car is running like eighteen,
BUT MY KNEES STILL HAVE MORE MILES

ROOM FOR RENT

Room for Rent in life's greatest vacancy,

With three windows, two facing Violet's Garden

And the third is blocked by a Flower Tree

The walls are all white with red trimming that shines

And there's a Queen Size Bed in the middle surrounded by,

White Wine Vines

Yes I have a Room for Rent,

Where life is easy in all of its senses

This is a place for the stars where every smile is meant,

And the air is filled with such a blissful scent that could never tart

Even though this vacancy is supposed to be,

Top secret and confidential

I think you'll be a perfect tenant to move inside thine heart

ONE HOUR

Use your imagination Baby to see what I can see

Close your eyes and use your heart to focus,

On nothing else but me

Let's play tag on top of Heaven's clouds,

Or Make Love beneath "King" Neptune's seas

When you're with my heart, Baby you can have the world;

And doing anything that your soul desires

I don't want to take up your whole day,

Just give me one hour

To show you in January the meaning of April showers,

The beauty of rainbows other people may stop to see

But the beauty that I can see deep inside of your eyes,

Makes everything else seem invisible to me

So come on My Queen one hour is all it takes,

To turn your norm into an hour…

FULL OF ECSTASY

YESTERDAY'S LOVE

Yesterday's Love was such an easy game to play,

Why My Love had to go?

I don't know, she just wouldn't stay

Suddenly, I'm not half the man that I used to be,

By not fighting for your love to remain within me

If I could had foreseen the pain that stains today,

My heart would go back in time to change yesterday

The pain absorbed up all the laughter, love and tears,

Which sat on the bay

And melted them all down like gold into a chain of clay

There's time in your life were you get what you want

But then the catch is, you'll miss what you need,

My lust cried for another, all due to greed

And now from the hole of yesterday,

My heart will incessantly bleed

PAST TIMES

Past times were so beautiful

I remember how you use to hold me tight,

Until I went to sleep

And every time after we sailed through passionate sex,

You would rub my feet through the night

It was like I was always in a daze,

Running around chasing your love inside of your heart's maze

Because I never thought I would love someone as deep as this,

I never thought you would have me on the first kiss

Who would have thought that I could love this person?

Better than my Ex?

I'm genuinely in love with this person in front of me,

FROM THE OPPOSITE SEX